Let's Get Crafty with
Paper
& Glue

Let's Get Crafty with Paper & Glue

FOR KIDS AGED 2 AND UP

CICO **kidz**

Published in 2016 by CICO Kidz
An imprint of Ryland Peters & Small Ltd
20–21 Jockey's Fields   341 E 116th St
London WC1R 4BW   New York, NY 10029

www.rylandpeters.com

10 9 8 7 6 5 4 3 2 1

Text © CICO Books 2016, plus the project makers listed on page 80
Design and photography © CICO Books 2016

A CIP catalog record for this book is available from the Library of Congress and the British Library.

ISBN: 978 1 78249 335 8

Printed in China

Editor: Katie Hardwicke
Designer: Eoghan O'Brien
Photographer: Terry Benson
Stylist: Emily Breen
Technique illustrators: Rachel Boulton and
Hannah George
For additional photography and styling credits,
see page 80

In-house editor: Dawn Bates
In-house designer: Fahema Khanam
Art director: Sally Powell
Head of production: Patricia Harrington
Publishing manager: Penny Craig
Publisher: Cindy Richards

Contents

Introduction

PAPER AND GLUE ARE THE PERFECT STARTING POINTS FOR GETTING CRAFTY WITH YOUNG CHILDREN—WITH SIMPLE, INEXPENSIVE MATERIALS, A LITTLE IMAGINATION, AND SOME CUTTING OUT HELP, THEY'LL BE CREATING TOYS, GIFTS, DECORATIONS, AND ARTWORKS THAT WILL GIVE THEM A HUGE SENSE OF ACHIEVEMENT, WITH LOTS OF FUN ALONG THE WAY.

Getting crafty is the ideal activity for rainy afternoons, mid-morning lulls, play dates, and party planning, and in this book you'll find plenty of ideas and inspiration for fun craft activities that you can make together.

For playtime fun, try the simple Paper-plate Frog on page 14, the Juice Box Boats on page 28, or take to the air with the Catapult Plane on page 56. Making party or festive decorations is a great way to keep over-excited little ones occupied; try the Paper Chains on page 26, or Paper Snowflakes on page 72 —all you need are paper, scissors, and glue. For celebrations, the Cupcake Toppers on page 40 are the perfect finish to an afternoon of baking, and the cones on page 42 are ideal for a party activity and favor all in one! Young children will be very proud of their creations, and several of the projects make charming gifts for them to present to loved ones; the Paper-mâché Bowl on page 60 is a lovely Mother's Day gift, and the Handprint Tree Picture on page 44 is a sweet way to preserve tiny handprints for grandparents to treasure.

Using scissors, pens, glue, paintbrushes, and simple paper folding construction are all great ways for young children to develop fine motor skills and coordination. While many projects will only need light adult supervision, there are some steps, marked with a helping hands symbol, that will require your help, either where the task is difficult or involves sharp objects, or where a guiding hand will ensure success. Encourage your child to attempt the tasks and they will soon learn and acquire confidence. Working as a team is all part of the fun and your child will enjoy spending time with you and learning from you, as you get crafty together.

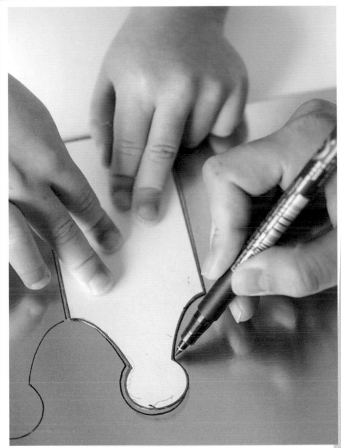

WHAT YOU WILL NEED

For all the projects you will need some basic craft materials. Keep a dedicated corner or drawer for storing your equipment, and stock up on a few craft materials for the finishing touches—a good supply of googly eyes is essential! Don't forget the recycling box—gift wrap, greeting cards, newspapers, cardboard boxes, plastic containers, and the like can all be transformed into fun creations with a little glue and imagination.

BASIC EQUIPMENT

- Pencils
- Ruler
- Eraser
- White construction paper
- Colored construction paper
- Card for templates
- Thin and thick card
- Tracing paper
- Craft scissors
- Sharp paper scissors
- Acrylic paints and paintbrushes
- Felt-tipped pens or marker pens
- Coloring pencils
- White/PVA glue
- Sticky tape
- Glue stick
- Paper plates
- Paper towels
- Toothpicks

CRAFT MATERIALS

- Glitter
- Sequins, gems
- Wooden or felt shapes
- Feathers
- Pom-poms
- Elastic bands
- Yarn
- Buttons, ribbons, braid, beads
- Pipe cleaners
- Googly eyes
- Cotton balls

RECYCLING BOX

- Gift wrap and greeting cards
- Tissue paper
- Newspapers and magazines
- Plastic containers
- Cardboard boxes, egg cartons, or cereal boxes
- Fabric scraps

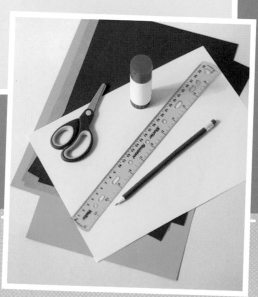

GETTING MESSY!

Much of the fun of crafting is the chance to get messy and to make some mess! Follow these tips before you begin for stress-free crafting:

- Cover your work table with newspaper or a wipe-down sheet or tablecloth.
- Protect your child's clothes with an apron or old T-shirt (you may want to do the same!).
- Roll up sleeves and tie long hair out of the way.
- Keep a roll of paper towels close by.
- When using glitter or sprinkles, put a sheet of paper or newspaper beneath the project and use it to pour the excess glitter back into the pot afterward.

CLEARING UP!

Ask your child to help to clear up afterward— washing up paintbrushes and pots will appeal to all those who love to play with water!

- Put all lids back on glue pots, paint pots and tubes, and felt-tipped pens.
- Wash paintbrushes and palettes; stand paintbrushes in a jar to dry.
- Throw away newspaper and wipe down surfaces.
- Throw away little scraps of paper but keep larger pieces for future activities, or put them in the recycling box.
- Put any equipment away in drawers or boxes to keep it organized and easy to find next time.

TECHNIQUES

CUTTING OUT

Using scissors to cut a straight line is a skill that most young children can master with children's craft scissors. However, several of the projects require you to cut out detailed shapes and we have suggested that an adult help with these stages, either guiding your child or cutting out yourself. Here are a few tips to make cutting out easier and safer:

• **Cutting rounded or detailed shapes:** hold the scissors steady in one place and let your other hand move the paper as you cut, rather than moving the scissors.

• **Cutting windows or holes:** to cut out a window or hole from the center of a shape, use the point of the scissors to pierce the paper in the center of the shape, cut a slit to the inner edge, then cut out around the inner edge to remove the shape.

• **Cutting circles:** some projects require you to cut circles. This is quite tricky for little hands, and even big hands: keep the scissors in one place and turn the paper as you cut, or alternatively draw around a button, bobbin, or other round object first to make a template, then cut out.

PAPER FOLDING

Some of the projects use paper folding techniques, such as as origami or concertina folds, which require quite precise folding and creasing, and will need adult assistance in order to be successful. However, children will love to make the creases and will soon master the folds.

ORIGAMI FOLDS

Here are some tips on basic origami techniques:

- When you make a fold, make sure that the paper lies exactly where you want it.
- As you make the crease, make sure that you keep the paper completely still so that the crease is straight.
- Still holding the paper, use a ruler or your fingernail to press down the fold until it is as flat as possible.

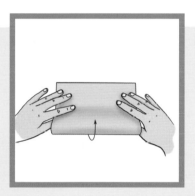
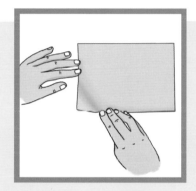
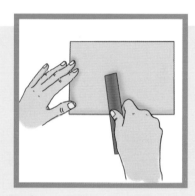

CONCERTINA FOLDS

These require a little teamwork in order to make even folds—here's how:

- Lay the sheets of paper on top of each other, making sure that they are all the same size and the edges are aligned.
- Fold all the layers over together by the amount required.
- Turn the pile of paper over and fold the layers over by the same amount again.
- Keep turning and folding until you have made a zigzag, or concertina, of folded paper.

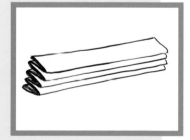

➤ MAKING TEMPLATES

For some projects you need to transfer the shape from the templates given on pages 76–79 onto card, before using it to cut out the final shape from the material used in the project. All the templates are given at full size but you can use a photocopier to enlarge or reduce the shape if you'd prefer a different size.

1 Once the template is the right size, place a sheet of tracing paper over the template outline and hold in place with masking tape. Trace over the lines with a hard pencil.

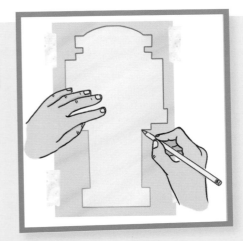

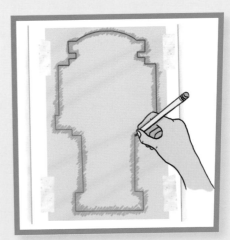

2 Turn the tracing paper over so that the back is facing you and neatly scribble over the lines with a softer pencil. Make sure all the lines are covered.

3 Turn the tracing paper over again so that the top is facing you and position it on your card, using masking tape to hold it in place. Carefully draw over the lines you made in step 1 with the hard pencil, then remove the tracing paper. The outline will be transferred to the card. Cut out the card template to use for your project.

4 Alternatively, you can photocopy the template directly onto thin card and cut it out.

▶ USING TEMPLATES

You may need to help your child when drawing around a template:

- Hold the template in place firmly.
- Use a pencil or marker pen to draw around the edge of the template onto the card or paper used in the project.
- Keep the pencil upright and draw a steady, continuous line.
- Use a white pencil on dark paper or card so that the outline will show clearly.
- On felt, a fine-tipped marker or felt-tipped pen may be easier to see.

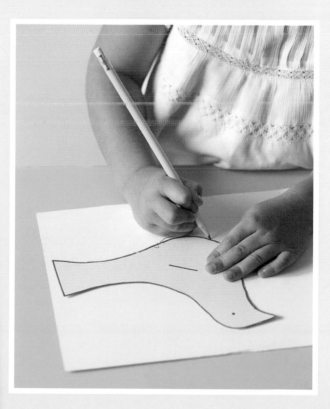

Paper-plate Frog

ALL FANS OF WIDE-MOUTHED FROGS WILL LOVE MAKING ONE OF THEIR OWN! WITH PAINTING, CUTTING, STICKING, AND FOLDING, THIS ACTIVITY IS PERFECT FOR LITTLE ONES TO GET FULLY INVOLVED.

WHAT YOU WILL NEED

- Paper plates
- Green acrylic paint
- Paintbrush
- Sticky tape
- Green pipe cleaners
- Template on page 79
- Card for template
- Pencil and scissors
- White/PVA glue
- Googly eyes
- Red card or construction paper

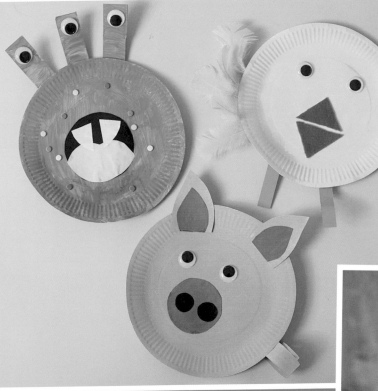

Crafty Tip

You can transform paper plates into all kinds of animals with different colored paint and simple cut out shapes.

1

PAINT PLATE Apply green paint to both sides of the paper plate using a large paintbrush. Cover the whole plate and let it dry completely. You may need to apply a second coat—use thin coats to help prevent the plate from buckling and wrinkling.

2

ADD LEGS Fold the plate in half. Use pieces of sticky tape to attach the pipe cleaner to the back of the plate, two on each side. Bend the legs into shape.

3

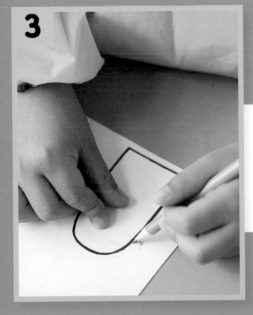

MAKE EYES Copy the eye template on page 79 and draw around the shape onto white card twice, and cut out.

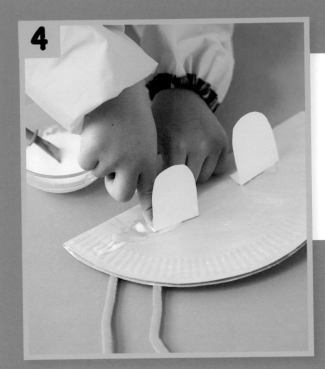

4

GLUE EYES Fold the base of the eyes and crease the fold. Apply glue to the underside and glue in place on the body, about ¾in (2cm) in from the back of the head.

ADD GOOGLY EYES Using a dab of glue, attach the googly eyes to the front of the eye shapes.

5

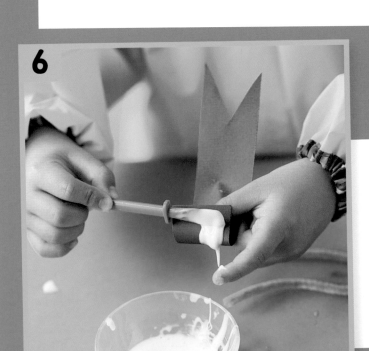

6

ADD TONGUE Cut out a thin, long rectangle from red paper or card for the tongue. Help your child to snip a triangle from the end and glue the tongue inside the mouth.

Stained-glass Butterflies

YOUNG CHILDREN WILL BE ENCHANTED BY THE EFFECT OF THESE STAINED-GLASS WINDOW SHAPES. WITH A LITTLE CUTTING, OR TEARING, THEY CAN HELP TO APPLY THE BRIGHTLY COLORED TISSUE PAPER PATCHES THAT TRANSFORM INTO BACKLIT PATTERNS WHEN HUNG AT A WINDOW.

WHAT YOU WILL NEED

- Template on page 78
- Paper or card for template
- Pencil and scissors
- Sheet of letter/A4-sized black construction paper or card for each shape
- White pencil
- Colored tissue paper
- White/PVA glue
- Black pipe cleaners
- Sticky tape (optional)

1

TRACE TEMPLATE Copy the template on page 78 and cut it out using scissors. Put the template on a piece of black paper then draw around it using white pencil (this makes the butterfly shape easier to see).

2

CUT OUT BUTTERFLY Use the scissors to cut out the butterfly shape from the black paper. If you are making more than one butterfly, it is easier to cut out all the shapes at once before cutting the holes and sticking on the tissue paper in the next steps.

DRAW SHAPES Using the white pencil, draw softly rounded shapes onto the back of the black paper butterfly. Use scissors to carefully cut out these shapes (make a hole in the center of each shape and cut out to the inner edge). These "windows" form the holes for the tissue paper.

TEAR TISSUE PAPER Cut out or tear pieces of tissue paper that are just slightly bigger than the "windows."

GLUE TISSUE PAPER Glue the tissue paper to the back of the butterfly shape over the windows. Use a tiny amount of glue, as too much will cause the tissue paper to get wet and tear.

ADD ANTENNAE Cut a black pipe cleaner in half and finish the butterfly with two antennae attached with blobs of glue or sticky tape on the back. Bend the ends a little.

Cardboard Bracelet

USING ZINGY COLORS AND LOTS OF PRETTY EMBELLISHMENTS, THESE BRACELETS WILL APPEAL TO LITTLE ONES WHO LOVE TO ACCESSORIZE! THIS ACTIVITY CAN BE MADE BY YOUNG CHILDREN ALMOST INDEPENDENTLY, WITH JUST A LITTLE CUTTING OUT HELP TO START WITH FOR THE VERY YOUNG.

WHAT YOU WILL NEED

- Cardboard tubes
- Scissors
- Ruler
- Acrylic paint
- Paintbrush
- Ribbon and ricrac braid
- White/PVA glue
- Flower shapes, buttons, sequins, glitter, to decorate

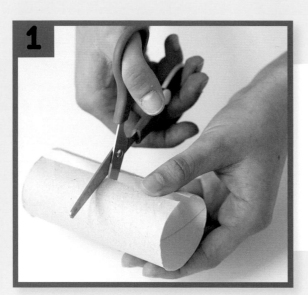

CUT OUT BRACELETS Cut open the cardboard tube in a straight line down its length using scissors. Then measure approximately 2in (5cm) in from the bottom of the tube and cut along this line to make a single bracelet.

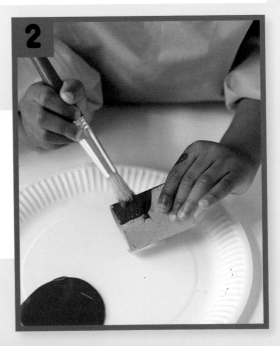

PAINT CARDBOARD Paint the cardboard roll both inside and out with your chosen color of paint and let it dry thoroughly. If you want a more solid color, apply a second coat of paint and let dry.

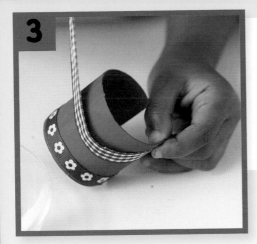

ADD RIBBON Cut the ribbon and ricrac braid to fit the circumference of the bracelet. Run a line of glue down each length of ribbon and braid and glue in place, pressing firmly in position to flatten any wrinkles out. Let dry completely.

DECORATE Once the glue is completely dry, stick a row of shapes around the top and bottom edge of the bracelet.

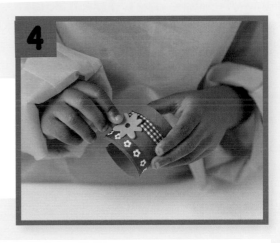

ADD SPARKLE Add dabs of glue where you would like some glitter. Put a sheet of paper on the work surface then sprinkle the glitter over the glue. Shake off the excess and pour it back into the container.

Crafty Tip

You could also paint patterns on the roll, such as flowers or spots, before decorating with buttons and braid.

Tissue-paper Flowers

DELICATE AND PRETTY, THESE DELIGHTFUL TISSUE-PAPER BLOOMS MAKE LOVELY GIFTS WHEN BUNCHED UP INTO A COLORFUL BOUQUET. LOOK OUT FOR MULTICOLORED PACKS OF TISSUE PAPER IN ART STORES, OR COLLECT LEFTOVER PIECES FROM PRESENTS AND PACKAGING TO HAVE ON HAND WHEN YOU NEED TO SAY IT WITH FLOWERS.

WHAT YOU WILL NEED

- Sheets of tissue paper in different colors
- Scissors
- Ruler
- Pipe cleaners
- Twigs

1

LAYER TISSUE PAPER Measure and cut 10 pieces of different colored tissue paper, 9½ x 12in (24 x 30cm). Lay them on top of each other.

2

FIRST CREASE Fold all the layers of paper over together by about 1¼in (3cm) and make a crease.

3

MAKE A CONCERTINA Continue to fold the tissue paper until the whole thing resembles a concertina.

4

SHAPE THE STRIP Cut both ends of the strip into either a curved petal shape or snip it into thin strips using scissors.

Crafty Tip

Make a few flowers in different colors to create a beautiful bouquet.

5

WRAP THE LAYERS Take a long pipe cleaner, fold it in half, and twist it around the middle of the paper strips.

MAKE PETALS Carefully pull each layer of paper out to form the petals.

6

7

ATTACH TO TWIG Twist the pipe cleaner onto the end of a twig. Add a leaf shape if you like.

Paper Chains

WHAT YOU WILL NEED
- Selection of colored paper, at least 11in (28cm) wide (letter/A4 size)
- Pencil, ruler, and scissors
- White/PVA glue or glue stick
- Paintbrush

PAPER CHAINS TRADITIONALLY APPEAR DURING THE WINTER HOLIDAYS, BUT THEY ARE PERFECT FOR ADDING A CELEBRATORY FEEL TO OTHER SPECIAL OCCASIONS, ESPECIALLY CHILDREN'S PARTIES. GET THE BIRTHDAY BOY OR GIRL TO HELP YOU MAKE THEM; THEY ARE SIMPLE AND CAN BE AS COLORFUL AS THEY LIKE.

1

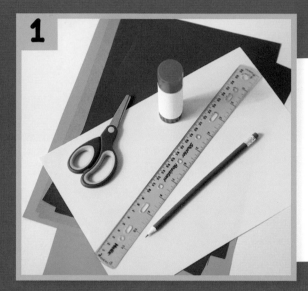

CHOOSE COLORS Ask your child what colors she or he would like to use to create the chains and make a pile of paper. For more decorative paper chains, you could use patterned gift wrap or translucent tracing paper, which is available from art stores in a variety of colors.

2

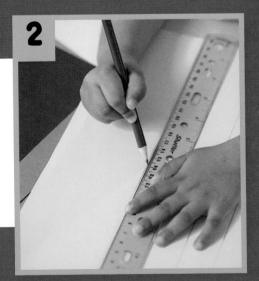

DRAW STRIPS Using a pencil and ruler, draw the strips on the back of the paper, making sure that each one is approximately ¾in (2cm) wide. A letter/A4-sized sheet of paper, used landscape, should give around 14 strips.

3

CUT STRIPS Using scissors, cut out the strips—slightly older children will enjoy doing this themselves. It is a good idea to keep the colors separate by making a pile of strips in each color, so they are easier to select when joining the chains together.

MAKE CHAINS Form a loop with the first paper chain and put a dab of glue on one end to stick it together. For the next link, thread the paper through the loop and glue the ends. Repeat to make more links, until you have made the required length of paper chain.

4

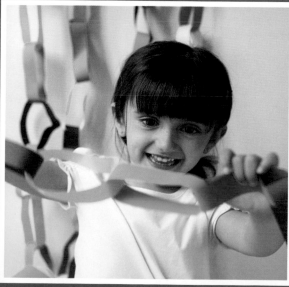

Juice Box Boats

RECYCLE JUICE CARTONS INTO COLORFUL SAILING BOATS FOR IMAGINATIVE WATER PLAY. THIS IS A GREAT ACTIVITY FOR A PLAY DATE, ESPECIALLY ON A RAINY DAY WHEN YOU CAN TAKE YOUR BOATS OUT TO RACE ON THE PUDDLES LEFT BEHIND AFTER THE CLOUDS HAVE CLEARED.

WHAT YOU WILL NEED

- Patterned paper
- Pencil and ruler
- Plastic cup
- 2 bamboo skewers
- White/PVA glue
- Empty juice box
- Sticky tape
- Scissors
- Modeling clay/Blu-Tack (optional)

MAKE SAILS On patterned paper, draw two rectangles measuring 3 x 6in (8 x 15cm), and cut them out. Place the plastic cup on the right-hand corner of one of the rectangles and draw a curved corner—do this to the other rectangle, too. Cut out the curved corners.

MEASURE FOLD Measure in by ½in (1cm) along the long edge of one of the rectangles, mark, and fold along the line.

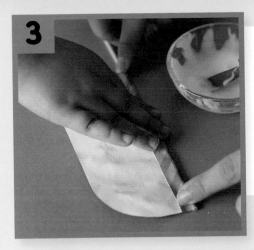

3

ATTACH SAIL Glue along the fold and press one of your bamboo skewers into the crease. Make sure the paper is positioned right at the top of your skewer. Do the same with the other rectangle and the other skewer.

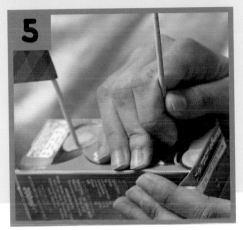

5

4 **TAPE BOX** Remove the straw from the empty juice box and use sticky tape to tape the hole shut securely.

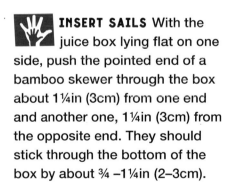

 **INSERT SAILS** With the juice box lying flat on one side, push the pointed end of a bamboo skewer through the box about 1¼in (3cm) from one end and another one, 1¼in (3cm) from the opposite end. They should stick through the bottom of the box by about ¾ –1¼in (2–3cm).

Crafty Tip

If your boat blows over, try sticking a small ball of modeling clay/Blu-Tack onto the bottom of the skewer to weight it down.

Ladybug Mobile

WHAT YOU WILL NEED

- Template on page 77
- Paper for template
- Pencil and scissors
- Sheet of red card
- Sheet of black card
- White/PVA glue
- White paint
- Paintbrush
- 2 wood battens measuring ½ x ½ x 8in (1 x 1 x 20cm)
- Red paint
- Drill or awl
- Nylon thread

LITTLE HANDS MAY NEED HELP CUTTING OUT THE LADYBUG'S SPOTS BUT THEY WILL LOVE CONSTRUCTING THIS CHEERFUL MOBILE TO DECORATE A WINDOW OR HANG ABOVE THEIR BED. YOU CAN USE BUTTONS OR STICKERS TO REPLACE THE SPOTS TO MAKE IT AN EVEN QUICKER MAKE, TOO.

 **CREATE TEMPLATE** Copy the ladybug template on page 77 twice and cut out. Draw around the body template on red card and around the face and spot templates on the black card. Draw a second set for the other side of the ladybug.

CUT OUT SHAPES Cut out the ladybug bodies, head, and spots. If preferred, you could use black self-adhesive dots or little buttons for the ladybug spots.

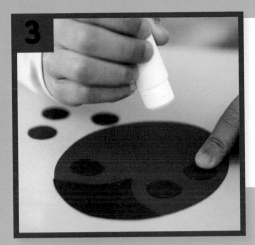

DECORATE LADYBUG Glue the face and six spots to one side of the ladybug, as shown. Turn over and repeat on the other side. Repeat these steps to make three more ladybugs.

PAINT EYES Use a paintbrush and white paint to paint on the eyes, or use small self-adhesive white stickers. Allow to dry completely.

5 **HANGING** Paint the wooden battens red and then drill a hole through the middle of each piece and at each end. Stick the battens together in the shape of a cross, lining up the central holes. Push through a loop of nylon thread to hang the mobile from. Make a hole at the top of each ladybug and use nylon thread to attach a ladybug to each of the four ends of the battens.

First Plane

PAPER PLANE CONSTRUCTION IS A GREAT INTRODUCTION TO ORIGAMI. WHILE YOUNG CHILDREN MAY NEED SOME HELP WITH MAKING THE FOLDS, THEY WILL LOVE RUNNING THEIR FINGERS ALONG TO SHARPEN THE CREASES, AND WILL BE DELIGHTED WHEN THE PLANE TAKES SHAPE AND IS READY TO LAUNCH.

WHAT YOU WILL NEED

- Sheet of letter/A4-sized construction paper
- Marker pens, stickers, pencils

1

FIRST FOLD Lay a piece of paper horizontally in front of you. Use a ruler to mark the center of the paper. Draw a faint guideline if necessary. Now fold one of the corners nearest you in to meet the guideline. Firmly press the fold. Repeat with the other corner and firmly press the fold flat with your finger.

FOLD LONG EDGES With the folds you made in step 1 uppermost, fold the long edges in once toward the central line and firmly press the folds flat.

2

3

4

✋ **FOLD FLAT** Turn the paper over, then fold it in half on itself (a valley fold) and press flat. This forms the basic shape of the airplane. Help your child to pinch the lower section of the "plane" between your fingers and open up the "wings," so they form a flat, horizontal surface.

DECORATE Turn the plane back over. You can decorate the wings of the aeroplane, if you like. Your plane is ready to fly!

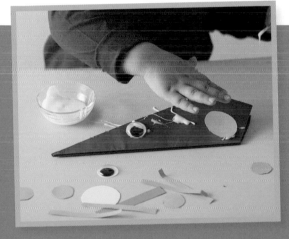

Crafty Tip
Don't use anything too heavy to decorate your plane—it may affect the aerodynamics!

Egg-carton Bugs

EGG CARTONS ARE INCREDIBLY VERSATILE CRAFT MATERIALS. HERE, THEY ARE TRANSFORMED INTO LONG-LEGGED ANTS WITH A LICK OF BROWN PAINT AND SOME LONG PIPE-CLEANER LEGS. WHY NOT ASSEMBLE A BUG COLLECTION WITH RED ANTS, GREEN GRASSHOPPERS, AND HAIRY SPIDERS, TOO?

WHAT YOU WILL NEED

- Egg carton
- Scissors
- Brown acrylic paint
- Paintbrush
- 4 brown pipe cleaners
- White/PVA glue
- 2 small paper-mâché beads
- Googly eyes
- Toothpick or bamboo skewer

PAINT EGG CARTON Use scissors to cut out two joined sections of the egg carton, assisting young children if necessary. Paint the carton using brown paint and let it dry completely. You may need to apply a second coat of paint for a more solid color.

GLUE ON LEGS Cut six equal lengths of brown pipe cleaner, each measuring approximately 4in (10cm). Glue three lengths of pipe cleaner along one side of the egg-box carton at equal spaces, then repeat on the other side. Bend the legs to adjust them so that the bug can stand up easily.

3

STICK ON EYES Paint the paper-mâché beads the same brown as the bug's body and let dry. Glue them to the front of the bug. Now glue a pair of googly eyes on top of the paper-mâché beads and allow to dry.

ADD ANTENNAE Use a toothpick or skewer to pierce two holes just above the eyes. Insert two lengths of pipe cleaner approximately 1½in (4cm) long. These are the antennae. If necessary, apply a blob of glue or sticky tape to the inside of the head to hold them in place.

4

Variation

Paint the carton black and add eight legs to make a spooky spider for Halloween!

Simple Flower Badge

BOLD AND BRIGHT, THIS SIMPLE FLOWER CAN BE USED TO ADORN CLOTHING, BAGS, SCOOTERS, OR DRESSING TABLES. QUICK AND EASY TO MAKE, A BUDDING FLORIST COULD HAVE A BUNCH FINISHED IN AN AFTERNOON—PERFECT AS A MOTHER'S DAY GIFT OR A THANK YOU GIFT FOR GRANNY.

WHAT YOU WILL NEED

- Template on page 76
- Card for template
- Pencil and scissors
- Colored card in different colors for the main flower shape and the flower centers
- Colored tissue paper or crêpe paper
- Glue stick
- Sticky tape
- Green pipe cleaner

1

COPY TEMPLATES Trace the flower templates on page 76 onto paper and cut them out. Draw around the main flower template on colored card and cut out the flower shape carefully, turning the paper, not the scissors, to cut the curved petals.

2

MAKE PETALS Use the petal template to cut out five petal shapes from crêpe or tissue paper in a contrasting color. Fold a small pleat in the bottom end of each petal.

3

GLUE PETALS Apply glue to the back of a petal and stick it in the center of a card flower petal. Repeat for each petal, then let the glue dry completely.

4

ADD FLOWER CENTER Draw around the flower center template on colored card and cut it out. Glue it to the center of the flower to cover the ends of the petals.

5

ATTACH STEM Use a small piece of tape to attach a pipe cleaner to the back of the flower to form a stem.

Crafty Tip

Use a button or foam shape for the center of the flower.

Royal Crown

THIS PROJECT IS GREAT FUN TO PUT TOGETHER, WITH LOTS OF CUTTING, GLUING, AND DECORATING, AND THE RESULT IS A DRESS-UP PROP THAT WILL STIMULATE IMAGINATIVE ROLE PLAY AND STORY-TELLING. USE ANY LEFTOVER FAKE FUR TO TRIM A REGAL CAPE FIT FOR ANY KING OR QUEEN.

WHAT YOU WILL NEED

- Template on page 78
- Card or cardboard and pencil
- Pencil or marker pen and scissors
- Large sheet of gold posterboard/card
- White/PVA glue
- Paper clips
- Fake fur
- Gold ricrac braid
- Fake jewels, gems, sequins, glitter, buttons, or beads, to decorate

1 TRACE CROWN Copy the template on page 78 for one section of the crown. Draw around it onto a piece of card or cardboard to make a strong template. Draw around your cardboard template ten times along the bottom edge of the gold posterboard, making sure that each section joins onto the one before.

CUT OUT Carefully cut out the crown along the top of the shape only, to make a continuous strip. Round shapes can be a little fiddly to cut; try turning the card rather than the scissors, as you cut.

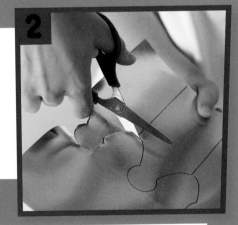

MAKE CROWN Bend the card strip into a circle, overlapping the ends slightly. Fix it together with paper clips and check that it fits over your head. Glue the overlapping ends together and replace the paper clips to hold it while it dries.

ADD FUR Cut a 22 x 1¼-in (56 x 3-cm) strip of fake fur. Spread glue around the bottom of the crown and glue the strip of fur in place, making sure that it is well stuck.

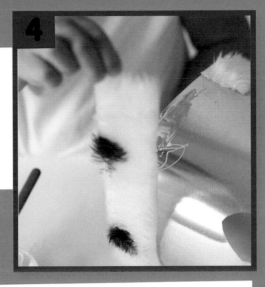

DECORATE Glue lengths of ricrac around the crown, overlapping the ends slightly at the back. Glue fake jewels or gems at intervals all the way around the crown, and add as much sparkly decoration as you like.

Cupcake Toppers

A PARTY TABLE ISN'T COMPLETE WITHOUT CUPCAKES AND THESE LITTLE TOPPERS ADD A COLORFUL FINISHING TOUCH. WE'VE MADE BOATS, WHICH USE SIMPLE SHAPES THAT YOUNG CHILDREN CAN CUT OUT EASILY, BUT YOU COULD ADAPT THE IDEA FOR ANY PARTY THEME—AND EVEN ADD NAMES TO MAKE PLACE MARKERS.

WHAT YOU WILL NEED

- Templates on page 79
- Card for templates
- Pencil and scissors
- Piece of card (you could use an old cereal packet)
- Scraps of patterned paper
- Glue stick
- Toothpicks

1

MAKE TEMPLATES Trace the topper templates on page 79 onto card. Draw around the shapes on patterned paper. Cut out a sail and two boat pieces for each topper.

GLUE SHAPES Fold the sail shapes in half. Spread glue on the inside. Stick the sail at the top of the toothpick, with the toothpick between the folded layers.

2

3

ADD BOAT Put glue on the inside of one of the boat shapes. Position the shape under the toothpick, beneath the sail, then stick the other boat shape on top so that the shapes match.

4 **INSERT TOPPERS** Stick the toppers in the cupcake frosting and remember to remove them before eating!

Party Bag Cones

PREPARING FOR A PARTY IS ALL PART OF THE FUN AND YOU CAN KEEP OVER-EXCITED LITTLE ONES BUSY BY HELPING TO MAKE THESE PARTY FAVOR BAGS. CHOOSE COLORS AND DECORATIONS TO MATCH THE PARTY THEME OR, FOR HALLOWEEN, USE BLACK OR ORANGE CARD AND FILL WITH CANDIES FOR TRICK OR TREATERS.

WHAT YOU WILL NEED

- 1 large plate to use as a template
- Pencil and scissors
- 12-in (30-cm) square piece of card for each cone
- Sticky tape
- White/PVA glue
- Sticky-backed felt animals or shapes for decoration
- Candies and chocolates, to fill

1

DRAW SEMICIRCLE Use the plate to draw a semicircle on the piece of card and cut out with scissors. You will need one semicircle of card for each cone. For each cone, you will also need to cut a handle measuring 1 x 8in (2.5 x 20cm) from the card.

2

ROLL INTO CONE Roll the card into a cone shape, making sure you hold the pointed end firmly with one hand. Use a piece of sticky tape to hold the cone in place.

ADD HANDLE Apply a dab of glue to one side of the inside of the cone and press one end of the handle in place. Repeat on the opposite side. Press down firmly with your fingers and allow the glue to dry.

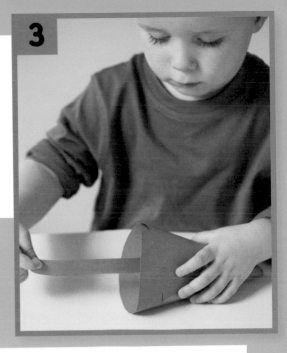

DECORATE Peel off the back of the felt animals and stick them on the cone. Or, you could color in the cone, or add stickers or buttons to decorate.

FILL WITH TREATS Fill the cones with yummy candies or chocolates, or small toys. Hand them out to your party friends.

Handprint Tree Picture

HANDS MAKE INSTANT TEMPLATES, WHETHER DUNKED IN PAINT AND PRINTED, OR DRAWN AROUND AS WE'VE DONE HERE TO MAKE A CUT-OUT PICTURE. THIS IS A GREAT WAY TO RECORD YOUR CHILD'S HANDPRINT—OR COMBINE THE WHOLE FAMILY'S HANDPRINTS TO MAKE A "FAMILY TREE." THERE'S PLENTY FOR LITTLE ONES TO GET INVOLVED WITH AND NO LIMIT ON THE AMOUNT OF DECORATIONS THEY CAN ADD TO THEIR PICTURE.

WHAT YOU WILL NEED

- Construction paper in assorted colors (a background color plus green, brown, red, orange, and yellow)
- Pencil and scissors
- Glue stick
- Stickers: flowers, apples, butterflies, ladybugs, or birds would all work well

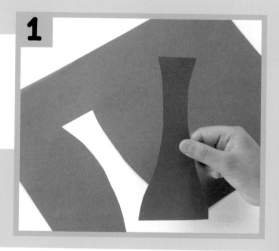

DRAW TRUNK Use a pencil to draw a tree trunk on brown construction paper. Cut out the tree trunk with scissors.

MAKE A HANDPRINT Choose a color of construction paper for the leaves (green, red, orange, or yellow). With the paper on a flat surface, put your child's hand on the paper and trace around it—remember to spread out the fingers! Repeat with the other hand so that you have two handprints on the paper. Using scissors, cut out the handprints; turn the paper not the scissors for the fiddly fingers.

MAKE THE PICTURE Choose a piece of colored construction paper for your background and start assembling your tree on the paper: glue down the tree trunk first and then the handprints (with the fingers pointing out as the leaves).

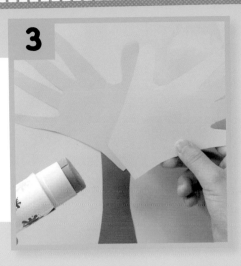

DECORATE Use stickers to decorate your tree— add as many as you want! You can even create little flowers next to the tree by drawing lines up from the bottom and putting a sticker at the top of each one.

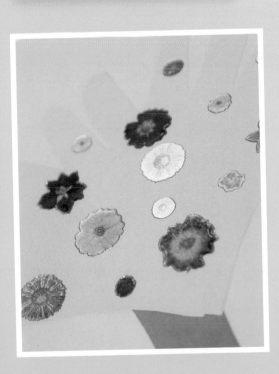

Cardboard Box Guitar

THIS PROJECT REQUIRES A LITTLE MORE ADULT INPUT, BUT YOUR CHILD WILL BE FASCINATED BY THE CONSTRUCTION AND DELIGHTED WITH THE MUSICAL RESULT! FOR BUDDING STARS, DECORATE IN DARK COLORS AND FLASHES OF GLITTER FOR GLAM ROCK COOL!

WHAT YOU WILL NEED
- Sturdy cardboard boxes
- Sticky tape
- Craft knife or scissors
- Thick card or cardboard
- Pencil and ruler
- Double-sided tape
- 12 paper fasteners
- 6 elastic bands
- Felt-tipped pens/markers or crayons

CUT HOLE Take a cardboard box and tape the openings shut. Using a craft knife or scissors, cut out a 3-in (8-cm) diameter hole, two thirds of the way down the face.

SCORE LINES To make the raised bridge, take a piece of cardboard measuring 5 x 2½in (12 x 6cm) and score three horizontal lines along the length with a ruler and pencil.

ADD BRIDGE Fold the card along the lines to make a raised ridge, as shown, and stick it to the box using the double-sided tape.

ADD FASTENERS Mark the position for the six paper fasteners on each end of the box, centered about ½in (1cm) below the top edge and spaced about ½in (1cm) apart. Push the paper fasteners through the box at the marked points.

ADD "STRINGS" Snip the elastic bands, then wrap one end around the first paper fastener. Pull the band to the paper fastener at the opposite end and wrap around again. Repeat with the remaining elastic bands.

FOLD NECK To make the neck, take a piece of card measuring 8 x 13¾in (20 x 35cm). Score three lines along the length, as you did in step 2, about 2¼in (5.5cm) apart. Fold the card to form a triangular prism and secure the overlapping edge with sticky tape.

7

INSERT NECK Using a craft knife or scissors, cut out a triangle with sides measuring 2in (5cm), from the top of the body. Slot in the guitar neck.

DECORATE Once your guitar is complete, your child can decorate it in their favorite colors. Cut out a guitar outline from paper, or use paint, paper, stickers, and gems to add star quality.

8

Crafty Tips

The tighter your elastic bands the clearer and higher the sound. It's essential to use a fairly strong box as otherwise it may collapse under the tension. Make sure there is enough space between the elastic bands so that they don't touch.

Snappy Crocodile

THIS CHEEKY CROCODILE WOULD MAKE A GREAT DECORATION IN A BEDROOM, READY TO BE PLAYED WITH OR JOIN IN WITH STORY-TELLING. WITH A LITTLE SIMPLE FOLDING, SOME GOOGLY EYES, AND A TOOTHY GRIN, IT IS EASY TO CREATE AND OFFERS LOTS OF OPPORTUNITIES FOR IMAGINATIVE DECORATION AND COLORING.

WHAT YOU WILL NEED

- Template on page 77
- Paper for template
- Pencil and scissors
- Sheet of letter/A4-sized green card or construction paper
- 2 googly eyes
- White/PVA glue
- White construction paper or card

1

COPY TEMPLATE Copy the template on page 77 and cut it out with scissors. Fold the green card or construction paper in half lengthwise and place the template on top, lining up the crocodile's spine with the fold of the card, as shown. Draw around the template and cut out.

SNIP SPINE Create the spiky spine effect by marking on the lines as indicated on the template. Snip along the lines through the fold of the card. Using a small pair of scissors will keep the cuts neat and tidy.

2

FOLD SPINE Open the crocodile out flat. The cuts will have created six triangular shapes. Fold these back on themselves, pressing them flat with your fingers. Carefully fold the crocodile in half again so that the knobbly spines stand up all the way along the crocodile's back.

ADD EYES AND TEETH Glue a googly eye to each side of the croc's head. Cut out a row of sharp teeth from white paper, and glue in place. Alternatively, paint the teeth with a fine paintbrush or use a piece of ricrac.

Crafty Tip

To give your croc's skin a rough pattern, try dipping a foam kitchen sponge in a little undiluted brown paint, and printing on the paper before cutting out in step 1.

Button Photo Frame

WITH A LITTLE PAINTING AND GLUING, THIS ACTIVITY BRINGS INSTANT RESULTS. PERSONALIZED PICTURE FRAMES MAKE LOVELY GIFTS—WE'VE MADE OURS WITH A CHRISTMAS THEME—AND YOU CAN EVEN EXTEND THE ACTIVITY BY DRAWING A PICTURE TO GO INSIDE.

WHAT YOU WILL NEED

- Plain wood picture frame
- Red or green acrylic paint
- Paintbrushes
- Assorted red buttons in different shapes and sizes, approx. ½in (1cm) in diameter
- White/PVA glue
- Colored pencils
- Paper

PAINT FRAME Paint the wood frame using your chosen color of paint and let it dry completely. If necessary, apply a further coat of paint for better coverage, then allow to dry completely.

GLUE BUTTONS Glue a button to each corner of the frame and press down firmly to make sure that they are securely stuck in place. You may wish to use buttons in an assortment of bright colors. Alternatively, mother-of-pearl buttons can look very pretty.

BUILD THE DESIGN Continue to glue on the rest of the buttons, working all the way around the frame and alternating different sizes and shapes. Press down hard on each button as you glue it in place to make sure that it is secure. Let dry completely.

DRAW PICTURES Use colored pencils to draw a picture to insert in the finished frame. For a holiday theme, Christmas trees, stars, bells, or Santas would all look great.

Variation

This idea can be used for any occasion: try pastel colors for a springtime theme; red hearts for Valentine's; or just your favorite colors to match bedroom décor.

Paper Birds

THESE PRETTY BIRDS MAKE PERFECT DECORATIONS FOR ALL KINDS OF OCCASIONS: PASTEL COLORS FOR SPRINGTIME; MULITCOLORED FOR BIRTHDAYS; OR IN SIMPLE WHITE FOR WEDDINGS OR CHRISTENINGS. YOUNG CHILDREN WILL LOVE ADDING EXTRA FEATHERS AND DECORATIONS FOR THE FINISHING TOUCHES.

WHAT YOU WILL NEED

- Template on page 76
- Paper for template
- Pencil and scissors
- Sheet of letter/A4-sized colored card
- Googly eyes, gems, stickers, craft feathers, to decorate
- White/PVA glue
- Sticky tape
- Squares of patterned or origami paper 6 x 6in (15 x 15cm)
- Black marker pen

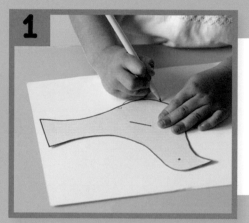

1

MAKE TEMPLATE Photocopy the bird template on page 76, marking on the position of the wing slit, then cut it out. Put the template on a piece of colored card and draw around it with a pencil.

2

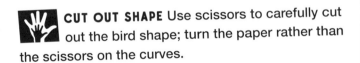

CUT OUT SHAPE Use scissors to carefully cut out the bird shape; turn the paper rather than the scissors on the curves.

3

DECORATE Glue some googly eyes onto the head and add some pretty plumage, either using craft feathers or with coloring pens, stickers, gems, or glitter. You can glue the feathers in place, or use a strip of sticky tape.

4

FOLD WINGS To make the wings, take a square of patterned paper. Starting at the end closest to you, make concertina-style folds that are approximately ¾in (2cm) wide. Press each fold flat.

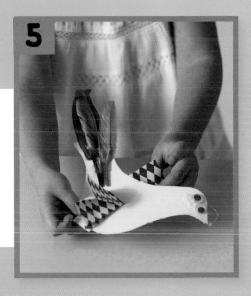

5

ADD WINGS To insert the wings, cut a slit on the bird's body where indicated on the template. Slide the folded wing section through the slit, then open out the pleats slightly to form the bird's wings.

Catapult Plane

ATTACHING A CATAPULT TO YOUR PAPER PLANE
ADDS AN EXCITING VARIATION TO THIS SIMPLE
PAPER FOLDING ACTIVITY. THIS IS A JOINT
PROJECT, AS MAKING PRECISE FOLDS IS CRUCIAL
FOR FLIGHT SUCCESS, THEN YOUR CHILD CAN
PERSONALIZE THEIR FINISHED PLANE WITH
STICKERS OR DRAWINGS. FIND AN OPEN SPACE
TO LAUNCH AND WATCH IT FLY!

WHAT YOU WILL NEED

- Sheet of paper, approx. 5¾ x 8¼in (A5), or half a sheet of letter/A4-sized paper
- Hole punch
- Elastic bands
- Stickers
- Wooden lollipop/craft sticks

1

FOLD CORNERS Fold the sheet of paper in half along the length. Run a fingernail along the crease to make a sharp edge, then unfold. Fold the top corners down so the points meet at the center crease, and then crease along the fold.

FOLD SIDES Fold the two long edges in against the center line as shown.

2

3

✋ **FOLD WINGS** Make a valley fold along the central line—fold together so that the folds made in step 2 are on the inside. Help your child create two wing creases on either side by folding the wings down, along the length of the paper plane, on each side.

4

MAKE HOLE Open the wings out flat. Punch a hole through the fold in the bottom of the plane, near the tip.

5

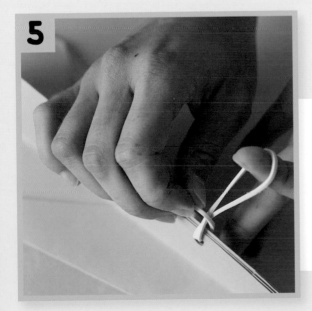

✋ **THREAD ELASTIC BAND** Pinch the sides of an elastic band together then push the looped end through the hole in the paper plane. Pull the other end of the rubber band through the loop and carefully pull tight.

DECORATE Embellish your plane with stickers or drawings. Just remember to avoid anything heavy or that might make the paper go soggy.

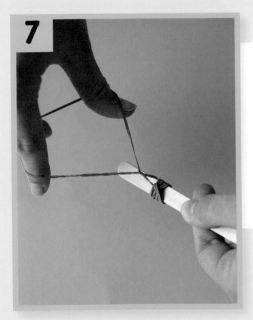

ADD LAUNCHER Wooden lollipop/craft sticks make great launchers. Wrap a different-colored elastic band around the top of the stick to act as a marker. Loop the plane's elastic band over the top of the stick, pull the plane back until the band is taut, and let go.

Crafty Tip

When it's time to launch your planes bear in mind that they can fire a long way. For best results (and to avoid any breakages or injuries), go outdoors!

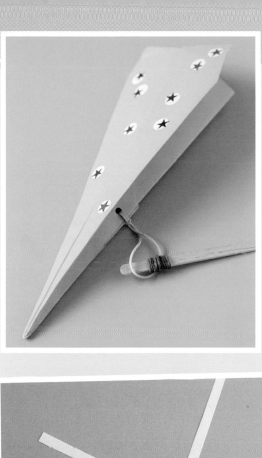

Paper-mâché Bowl

TIME TO GET MESSY! LITTLE ONES WILL LOVE THE CHANCE TO TEAR, DIP, AND STICK TO MAKE THEIR OWN PAPER-MÂCHÉ BOWL. THE FINISHED BOWL WOULD MAKE A LOVELY GIFT, OR KEEP IT FOR STORING BEDROOM BITS AND BOBS—MATCH THE COLORS TO THE BEDROOM DÉCOR.

WHAT YOU WILL NEED

- Plastic bowl (a mixing bowl is a good size)
- Petroleum jelly
- Plastic wrap/cling film
- Old newspaper
- White/PVA glue, bowl, and water
- Scissors
- Acrylic paint
- Paintbrush
- Scraps of gift wrap

1

PREPARE BOWL Cover the underside of a plastic bowl from the kitchen, such as a mixing bowl, with a layer of petroleum jelly and a piece of plastic wrap/cling film.

TEAR NEWSPAPER Tear some sheets of newspaper into strips. Using small strips will create a smoother finish.

START TO GLUE Pour some glue into a bowl and add water to dilute it so that it looks like light/single cream. Dip the newspaper into the glue and start to paste the pieces onto the bowl. Continue to put newspaper onto the bowl, making about three layers of paper. Let the bowl dry completely.

TRIM BOWL Remove the paper-mâché bowl by peeling away the plastic wrap/ cling film. Trim any uneven pieces around the edge with scissors, helping younger children if necessary.

5

PAINT BOWL Mix up some paint and use a generous amount to paint the inside and outside of the bowl. You may need two coats of paint for an even coverage—leave to dry between coats.

6

DECORATE Cut out flower and leaf shapes from gift wrap and glue onto the inside and outside of the bowl with undiluted white/PVA glue. To give the bowl a shiny finish, brush undiluted white/PVA all over it and let it dry.

Jar Lid Magnets

YOUNG CHILDREN LOVE MAGNETS—YOUR FRIDGE IS PROBABLY COVERED IN THEM BUT YOU'LL HAVE TO MAKE ROOM FOR THESE HOMEMADE VERSIONS, OR GIVE THEM AS GIFTS OR PARTY FAVORS. A SIMPLE ACTIVITY WITH FUN RESULTS, JAR LID MAGNETS CAN BE ADAPTED FOR ANY OCCASION.

WHAT YOU WILL NEED

- Old magazines, pictures printed from a computer, gift wrap, or greeting cards
- Scissors
- Metal jar lids
- White/PVA glue
- Container for mixing glue
- Paintbrush
- Magnets (available from craft stores)

1

FIND PICTURES Go through old magazines, gift wrap, or greeting cards and look for pictures or patterns that your child likes. They will need to fit on top of the jar lids so don't choose anything too big. Trace around the jar lid over your chosen pictures and cut them out with scissors.

MIX GLUE Pour one teaspoon of glue into a container. Add a teaspoon of water and stir well to mix. This will make a small amount of découpage glue—if you want to make a lot of magnets, you will need to mix up more glue. Just use equal quantities of glue and water and mix well.

ADD GLUE Using a paintbrush, brush a layer of the glue/water mixture on top of the metal jar lid. You can découpage either side of the lid—it's up to you.

GLUE PICTURE Next, put your picture cut-out on top of the glued side of the metal lid. Brush another layer of the glue/water mixture on top of the cut-out (don't worry—it will dry clear). Be sure to brush the edges and press in place to ensure the edges are attached to the lid.

5

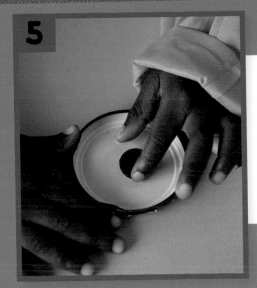

ADD MAGNET Allow the jar lid to dry—this may take up to an hour. When the lid is dry, glue a magnet to the other side of the lid.

MAKE MORE! This is such a quick activity that you won't want to stop at one magnet! Make a collection and dedicate some fridge space for displaying them all.

6

Paper Wreath Crown

USING HANDS AS STENCILS GIVES THIS FUN PROJECT INSTANT APPEAL. WITH GLUING AND STICKING GALORE, THERE'S LOTS OF OPPORTUNITY FOR GETTING CREATIVE. WE'VE MADE OUR WREATH CROWN IN BRIGHT COLORS, BUT YOU COULD TRY USING METALLIC CARD WITH GLITTERY ACCESSORIES FOR A FAIRY EFFECT, OR PLAIN GREEN PAPER FOR AN AUTHENTIC ROMAN EMPEROR'S WREATH!

WHAT YOU WILL NEED

- Construction paper in lots of colors
- Pencil or pen
- Scissors
- Sheet of letter/A4-sized card
- Glue stick
- Stickers for fingernails and rings
- Paper clips (optional)

1

TRACE HAND With the paper on a flat surface, put your child's hand on the paper and trace around it— remember to spread out the fingers! Round off the base at the wrist.

CUT OUT HAND Cut out the hand shape; turning the paper not the scissors will help on the fiddly curves. Continue to trace and make hands in different colors. We used ten hands to make the wreath shown here, but you could use more or fewer depending on your child's head size.

2

3

MAKE THE CROWN BASE Take the card and, using scissors, cut out two strips 1½in (4cm) wide along the long side of the card. Glue them together with a 1-in (2.5-cm) overlap to make a long strip. Wrap the strip around your child's head, trim to fit, and mark where the two ends overlap with a pencil.

ADD HANDS Take a paper hand and glue the palm of the hand onto the crown base—don't glue the fingers down. Glue the next hand so that the fingers overlap the back of the first hand. Repeat with the rest of the paper hands until you have covered the base. Have fun sticking on fingernails and rings to decorate the hands.

FINISH When everything is dry, fold the strip around, overlap the ends, and glue the strips together to form the crown shape. You may need to add paper clips to hold the ends in place while the glue dries.

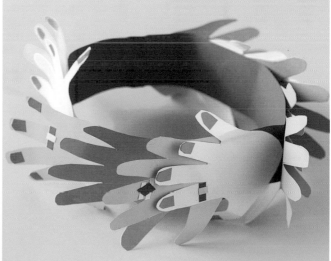

Angel Tree Topper

DECORATING THE TREE IS ALL PART OF THE BUILD-UP TO THE CHRISTMAS FESTIVITIES. HERE'S A GREAT EXCUSE TO GET OUT THE GLITTER AND MAKE A SUITABLY SPARKLY ANGEL TO TAKE PRIDE OF PLACE ON TOP OF THE TREE, OR YOU COULD MAKE SEVERAL AND LINE THEM UP ON THE MANTELPIECE OR HANG AT THE WINDOW.

WHAT YOU WILL NEED

- 10-in (25-cm) diameter plate as template for cone
- Silver card
- Pencil and scissors
- White/PVA glue
- Silver glitter
- Stapler
- Silver pipe cleaner
- Pom-pom for head
- Blue and pink 3-D fabric pens for face
- Gold pipe cleaner

DRAW SEMICIRCLE Put the plate on the silver card and draw around half of it to create a semicircle for the cone. Cut out the semicircle.

SPRINKLE GLITTER Use glue to draw a wavy line all around the curved edge of the semicircle. Put the card on a spare piece of paper or newspaper. Sprinkle silver glitter over the glue and leave for a few minutes. Shake off any excess glitter and return it to the container. Let the sparkly glue dry completely.

MAKE CONE Form the card semicircle into a cone shape (folding it gently in half and making a slight crease at the center of the card makes it a bit easier). Use a stapler to join the card together, or glue it and hold it in place with clothes pins/pegs while the glue dries.

MAKE WINGS Use the silver pipe cleaner to form the wings. Twist the ends over to form a figure eight.

5

ATTACH WINGS Apply a dab of glue to the center of the wings and glue them to the back of the cone, about 1¼in (3cm) down from the top. Allow the glue to dry completely.

6

ADD HEAD Glue a pom-pom to the top of the cone and let it dry. Use 3-D fabric pens in pink and blue to draw the angel's eyes and mouth on the pom-pom. Let it dry.

7

ADD HALO For a halo, bend a gold pipe cleaner into a circular shape with a diameter of about 1¼in (3cm). Twist the ends together to secure, and glue it to the top of the pom-pom head to finish. Proudly put your angel on the top of the tree!

Crafty Tip

Use red card to make a Santa tree topper complete with a cotton-ball beard or a Rudolph the Reindeer tree topper using brown card and a pair of pipe-cleaner antlers!

Paper Snowflakes

CHILDREN ARE ENCHANTED BY SNOWFLAKES AND WILL BE THRILLED TO UNFOLD THEIR OWN CREATIONS. WITH A LITTLE FOLDING AND CUTTING, THEY ARE EASILY MADE FROM PAPER, TISSUE PAPER, OR TRACING PAPER. THEY LOOK GREAT STUCK TO WINDOWS, STRUNG ACROSS A ROOM AS BUNTING, OR SUSPENDED FROM LENGTHS OF THREAD FOR A SNOWSTORM EFFECT.

WHAT YOU WILL NEED
- Sheets of white construction paper, about 8in (20cm) square for a large snowflake, or 4in (10cm) for a small snowflake
- Pencil and scissors

FOLD PAPER Take a square piece of paper. Fold it in half diagonally to form a triangle, run your fingers along the crease. Then fold in half again and then into quarters. You should now have a small folded triangle shape.

DRAW DESIGN Using a pencil, draw triangular or scalloped shapes on the folded edges of the paper. You can draw curved shapes on the top edges of the paper (farthest from the center), too. Experiment with different shapes, so that all your snowflakes are slightly different.

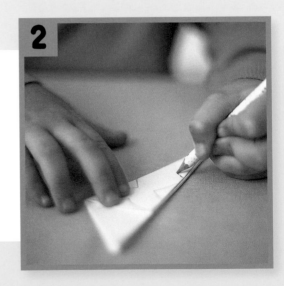

3

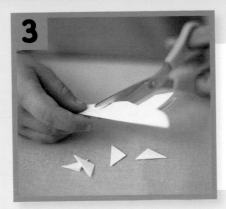

🖐 **CUT OUT** Carefully cut along the lines you have drawn on the paper; young children may need a little help cutting small shapes. The more shapes you cut out, the more decorative and delicate the finished snowflake will be.

4

UNFOLD Gently unfold the paper and carefully press it flat to reveal the snowflake's design.

Crafty Tip

You can leave the snowflakes as pure white or add glitter and sparkles for a frosty effect.

Walnut-shell Boats

THESE LITTLE BOATS ARE A QUICK ACTIVITY AT ANY TIME OF YEAR. YOU CAN TAKE THEM TO YOUR NEAREST STREAM FOR THEIR MAIDEN VOYAGE, A ROCK POOL AT THE BEACH OR, IF YOU WANT TO STAY CLOSER TO HOME, THE DISH-WASHING BOWL WILL DO JUST FINE!

WHAT YOU WILL NEED

- Whole walnuts
- Knife or nutcracker
- Sheet of patterned paper
- Pencil, ruler, and scissors
- Hole punch (optional)
- Toothpick/wooden skewer (cut into 3-in/8-cm lengths)
- Modeling clay/Blu-Tack

1

SEPARATE WALNUT Using a knife or nutcracker, carefully split some walnuts in two. Try to split the nut around the middle where there is a raised ridge; this way, the nut should crack neatly into two halves.

CUT PAPER SAILS Cut strips of paper 1½in (4cm) wide. Measure 2in (5cm) along the strip and cut out a rectangle. Repeat to make as many sails as required.

2

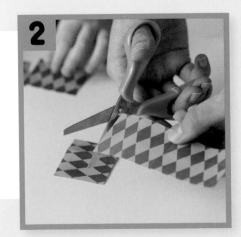

3

MAKE THE SAIL Take a small rectangle of paper and either punch a hole at either end, about ¼in (5mm) in from the edge, or push the toothpick through to make a hole. Now gently thread the paper onto the toothpick, watching out for the sharp end.

ATTACH MODELING CLAY Roll a ball of modeling clay that's small enough to fit into a walnut half and push this onto one end of the toothpick.

4

5

SET SAIL Push the modeling clay ball firmly into the base of a walnut shell. Roll a small piece of modeling clay and cover the sharp point at the top of the mast. Now you're all ready to go sailing!

Templates

For help on using templates, see pages 12–13.
All the templates are printed at actual size.

SIMPLE FLOWER
BADGE: PETAL

Paper Birds

PAGE 54

Simple Flower Badge

PAGE 36

Ladybug Mobile

PAGE 30

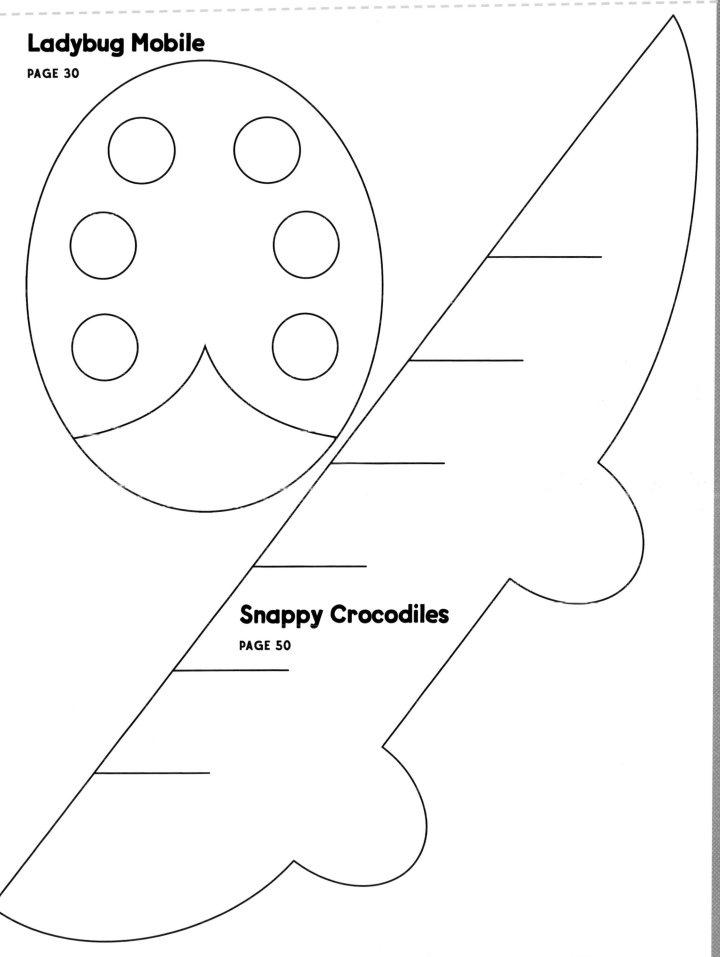

Snappy Crocodiles

PAGE 50

Stained Glass Butterflies

PAGE 17

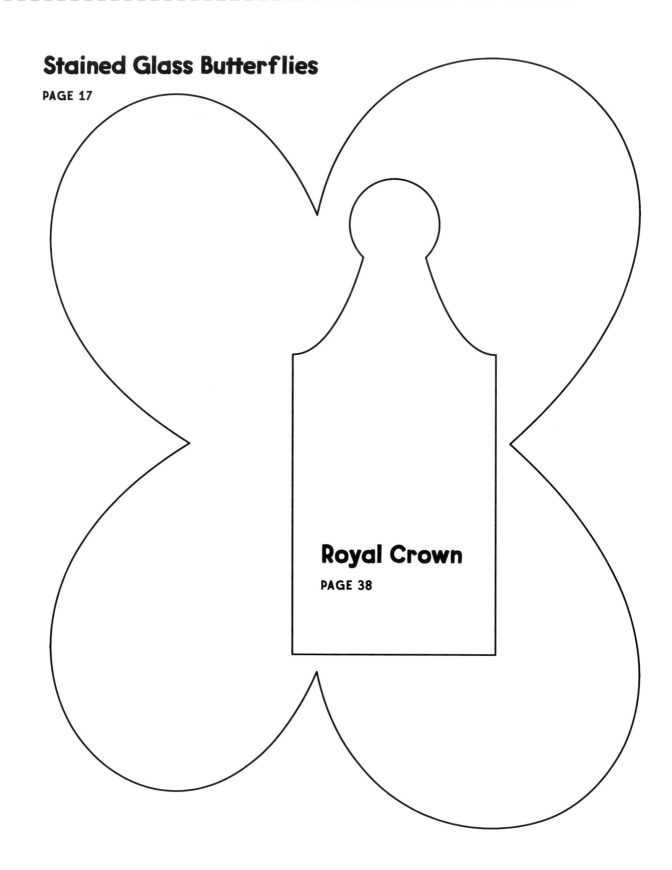

Royal Crown

PAGE 38

Paper-plate Frog

PAGE 14

Cupcake Toppers

PAGE 40

Suppliers

US

A C Moore
www.acmoore.com

Create for Less
www.createforless.com

Creative Kids Crafts
www.creativekidscrafts.com

Darice
www.darice.com

Hobby Lobby
www.hobbylobby.com

Jo-ann Fabric & Crafts
www.joann.com

Michaels
www.michaels.com

Mister Art
www.misterart.com

Walmart
www.walmart.com

UK

Baker Ross
www.bakerross.co.uk

Early Learning Centre
www.elc.co.uk

Hobbycraft
www.hobbycraft.co.uk

Homecrafts Direct
www.homecrafts.co.uk

John Lewis
www.johnlewis.co.uk

Mulberry Bush
www.mulberrybush.co.uk

Paperchase
www.paperchase.co.uk

The Works
www.theworks.co.uk

Yellow Moon
www.yellowmoon.org.uk

Index

CREDITS

Key: t = top, c = center,
b = bottom, l = left, r = right

PROJECT MAKERS

Libby Abadee and Cath Armstrong:
pp. 2br, 3bl, 28–29, 66–67
Emily Breen: pp. 2bl, 32–33
Caroline Fernandez: pp. 44–45, 63–65
Emma Hardy: pp. 7tr, 22–25, 38–39, 60–62
Kate Lilley: pp. 2tr, 3br, 10t, 46–49,
56–58, 74–75
Catherine Woram: pp. 1, 2tl, 3tl, 4, 5b,
7, 10b, 14–21, 26–27, 30–31, 34–37,
42–43, 50–55, 68–73
Clare Youngs: pp. 5t, 40–41

PHOTOGRAPHY

Carolyn Barber: pp. 2tr, 47tr, 49bl,
58tr, 58b
Terry Benson: pp. 1–7, 8b, 9t, 10, 13–21,
23bl, 25, 26–29, 32–33, 36–39, 40–43,
46–49, 50–51, 54–58, 63–67, 74–75
Martin Norris: pp. 44–45
Debbie Patterson: pp. 22–24, 39bl, 60–62
Claire Richardson: p. 9b
Tino Tedaldi: p. 8tr
Polly Wreford: pp. 4t, 7bl, 17tl, 30–31,
34–35, 51cl, 52–53, 55br, 68–73

STYLING

Liz Belton: pp. 2tr, 47tr, 49bl, 58tr, 58b
Emily Breen: pp. 1–7, 8b, 9t, 10,
13–21, 26–29, 32–33, 36–43,
46–51, 54–58, 63–67, 74–75
Emma Hardy: pp. 22–25, 39bl, 60–62
Sophie Martell: pp. 44–45
Catherine Woram: pp. 4t, 7bl, 9t, 13, 17tl,
51cl, 52–53, 55br, 68–73
Clare Youngs: pp. 9b, 13bl

ILLUSTRATORS

Rachel Boulton: pp.11tl, 11tc, 11tr, 12
Hannah George: p.11